UNITED KINGDOM READING ASSOCIATION

MINI BOOK SERIES
No. 3

Miscue Analysis in the Classroom

Robin Campbell

Mini Book Series

No. 3

Series Editor: Alison B. Littlefair

Issue No. 3: **Miscue Analysis in the Classroom**

Author: Robin Campbell

ISBN: 1 897638 02 7

Published by: United Kingdom Reading Association
°/o Warrington Road County Primary School, Naylor Road, Widnes,
Cheshire WA8 0BP, England.

July 1993

British Library Catalogue in Publication. A catalogue record for this book is available from the British Library

Contents

WHO IS THIS BOOK WRITTEN FOR?

First, and importantly, the book is written for teachers and students who want to learn about their pupil's reading development from the miscues/errors/mistakes that those children make as they read orally. But also it is for those teachers and students who know something about miscue analysis but who wish to extend that knowledge and do so within a short text devoted entirely to the subject.

WHY IS KNOWLEDGE ABOUT MISCUES IMPORTANT?

• We recognise that children produce miscues as they read.
• Miscue analysis provides us 'with a window on the reading process' (Goodman, K., 1973).
• An understanding of miscue analysis can enable us to become more analytic listeners to children's reading.
• Miscue analysis enables us to become more sophisticated in our response to children's miscues.
• A detailed knowledge of miscue analysis enables us to assess and diagnose a child's reading.
• The diagnosis derived from miscue analysis enables us to plan literacy programmes and teaching strategies for the child.

WHY MISCUES?

In the opening section I referred to the miscues/mistakes/errors that children make as they read. So why do we choose to talk about the miscues rather than the mistakes or errors?

The term miscue presents a positive view of the child as a reader; mistakes/errors have more negative connotations. The positive terminology, miscue, recognizes that the child is using his/her knowledge of language and personal experiences to read the text. The child's miscues, then, are derived from placing too great an emphasis upon one of the language cue systems and therefore miscueing.

5

Nevertheless the child is demonstrating strengths when a miscue is produced and an analysis of the miscues indicates the knowledge and strategies of the reader. (The language cue systems - semantic, syntactic or graphophonic - are terms which we will explore in greater detail shortly.)

Those readers of this text who already have some knowledge of miscue analysis will be aware of the debt that we owe to Kenneth Goodman for his major part in developing the theoretical aspects of miscue analysis and I have drawn your attention earlier to one of his many articles (Goodman, 1973). Additionally, Yetta Goodman, with two colleagues, has developed the complex and highly detailed miscue inventories (Goodman, Watson and Burke, 1987) which form the basis for much of our more simplified discussion of miscue analysis. And as a first step in any miscue analysis we need to be able to recognise and describe the miscues that are produced by a reader during an oral reading. Therefore, we should look now at the collection and description of miscues.

COLLECTING MISCUES

In an ideal situation, and for a formal and diagnostic miscue analysis, the material that would be read by the child would be one which was new to them and complete with a beginning, middle and end. It would also be of sufficient length and difficulty to produce about 25 miscues, perhaps therefore of about five hundred words in length. Or for a younger child two or three shorter texts might be used over a matter of days. And the children would have been informed before starting that they should read in order to be able to retell the story/text and they would get no help as the session was to see how well they were getting on with their reading. Of course, if a child hesitates in front of a word for an extended period (e.g. thirty seconds) then some support might be given by telling the word, or suggesting that the child moves on to the next word. Normally an audio recording of the reading would be used as it can be very helpful for subsequent analysis. However, some teachers find that they are able to code the miscues directly onto a duplicate of the text. Subsequently that coded miscue sheet can provide the basis for an assessment of the child's reading.

For many teachers of young readers, collecting miscues may occur occasionally in the more formal manner indicated above but more frequently as part of every day teaching. Each time that the teacher shares a book with a child or hears them read then the miscues that are produced give the teacher some indication of the strengths and strategies of the reader. They do so because teachers ask of themselves "Why did the reader produce that miscue?". Providing that the teacher has a sound knowledge of miscues and miscue analysis then each listening adds to the understanding that the teacher has of the child as a reader. So what kind of miscues are produced by the readers?

DESCRIBING MISCUES

Let us look at a short piece of text in order to explore the kind of miscues that readers produce:

The dog got/wet (and) Tom had to//rub him dry.

In this example, drawn from the miscues that children have made on that sentence - although not necessarily at the same time - there were six miscues:

1. substitution	*down (for the text word 'dry')*
2. insertion	*in (added to the sentence after 'got')*
3. omission	*and (left out during the reading)*
4. repetition	*to-to (the word spoken more than once)*
5. hesitation	*// (a pause longer than three seconds)*
6. self-correction	*run-rub (initial attempt is corrected)*

Although it is accepted that there are many ways of categorizing the miscues that are produced, nevertheless for classroom purposes, those six miscues, I have argued elsewhere, (Campbell, 1988) do seem to be helpful. Nevertheless there are other miscues that you may need to consider. For instance in some classrooms I noted teachers might find a seventh category to be useful:

7. *sounding-out*   */d/og/-dog (reader sounds out the word)*

Additionally Helen Arnold (1984) included reversals and non-response in her listing:

8. *reversal*   *of words i.e. They so did - They did so.*
                 of letters i.e. was - saw

The reversal miscue will occur relatively infrequently and some teachers find it sufficient to regard a reversal of letters as a substitution. However, it is important to consider whether for a particular child the reversal is a frequent occurrence.

9. *non-response*   *where the text word is not read*

Dependent upon where such a miscue occurs the non-response might be regarded as an omission or a lengthy pause/hesitation.

Yetta Goodman and colleagues have further categories of:
10. *partials*   *The man left the por (porridge)*
11. *nonword*   *The gian (giant)*

In each of those instances the miscue can also be regarded as a substitution and coded as such. Subsequently during any analysis that takes place the teacher can consider the extent to which nonwords are appearing and what that might suggest for the future reading experiences of the reader. A further type of substitution which might be of interest would be those which reflect the reader's dialect:

12. *dialect*   *these can be marked as a substitution with the addition of a circled (d) to indicate dialect.*

In a more formal miscue analysis, and for particular purposes, all twelve of the miscues indicated above may be used in a coding of a child's reading. However, many teachers, working in a classroom context, may find that the first six categories of miscues (substitution, insertion, omission, repetition, hesitation and self-correction) will most usefully suit their needs and purposes.

COUNTING THE MISCUES

Describing and subsequently analysing the miscues that are produced by a reader will be the major interest for a teacher. However there is, also, a lesser need to consider the number of miscues that are produced. Earlier I suggested that perhaps 25 miscues would be required in order to provide an adequate assessment of the readers' strengths and weaknesses. That quantity of miscues might be produced, in one formal diagnostic reading, from about five hundred words of text. Therefore the reader would have an accuracy rate of approximately 95%. Of course in many readings the reader would vary slightly from that accuracy rate by a few percentage points. But what if the variation is more substantial?

In a formal miscue analysis the reader will be reading from a previously unread text. If the reader makes very few miscues (99% accuracy, say) then an analysis will not be feasible on such limited evidence. Or if the reader finds the text very difficult (less than 80% accurate perhaps) and is unable, therefore, to read independently then the miscues which are produced will less adequately reflect the reader's abilities. In such circumstances a different text may be required to complete the miscue analysis.

During normal shared readings in the classroom, where informal miscue analysis is taking place, then the teacher will still be interested in the number of miscues being produced. However, the interest will now serve a different purpose. If there are very few miscues the reader may be enjoying the text, but is the child's reading being developed? If too many miscues, is the reader being frustrated? Those questions might lead the teacher to encourage the child towards other books.

Of course, during this normal teaching activity of shared reading it is the cumulative analysis which is important. Therefore it is not necessary to acquire 25 miscues/substitutions in one reading. Over a longer period of weeks and months the child will produce many hundreds of miscues. Those miscues will demonstrate the changing strategies of the child. All that will help the teacher to make a continuing diagnosis.

THE IMPORTANCE OF SUBSTITUTIONS

Although each of the miscues that are produced provide some information about the reader, nevertheless it is the substitutions which are especially useful to the teacher. Those substitutions are important for at least three reasons.

First, substitutions occur most frequently in the miscues produced by readers. As many as 80% of miscues that are produced are likely to be those of substitution. Of course, some readers will, at various times, produce different patterns of miscues but overall the substitution will dominate.

Second, the substitution is the miscue which provides most information about the readers' strengths and weaknesses. After all the substitution (observed response) can be compared in detail with the text word (expected response). Insertions, omissions, hesitations etc, while giving information about the reader's strategies and thinking, do not allow for the same level of analysis.

Third, the analysis of substitutions, it follows from the above two points, produces a more detailed picture of the reader. Indeed it might be argued that such is the information provided by substitutions that during a formal miscue analysis a teacher might want to have not just 25 miscues to analyse but 25 substitutions.

However, before we consider in detail the way in which those substitutions can be analysed we should look at the information which the other miscues provide and the positive and negative aspects of those miscues.

POSITIVE AND NEGATIVE ASPECTS OF MISCUES

Each miscue that is noted can provide important insights into the child as a reader. And each miscue might indicate positive or negative features of the child's reading. Let us consider briefly each of the six main categories:

Substitutions; the miscue will be seen as positive where the child is actively processing the syntactic, semantic and graphophonic cueing systems and the substitution demonstrates that to be the case. However, if the reader does not appear to be using those cue systems, or perhaps is consistently using only one cue system then that might be regarded more negatively. That negative view might especially appertain where the reader was over-reliant upon the graphophonic cues rather than upon meaning.

Insertions and omissions; children will often demonstrate their strengths as readers with the insertions and omissions that they produce. In particular they will often appear to be acting as an editor of text when they produce those miscues either improving the text (!) or changing it into their dialect. However, in each case they will be demonstrating positively their understanding of the text. Occasionally, more negatively, the omissions will be of words that they find difficult and which they are reluctant to attempt. At times that will even lead to complete lines being omitted.

Repetition and hesitation; very often these miscues are used by children in order to buy time to consider the next word, or phrase, in the text. As such they are demonstrating involvement with the text and their positive attempts at reading. Of course, these miscues can have a negative influence if they occur too frequently. Is that the child's problem or the text's? Asking children to read a different story can change the nature of the miscues that they produce.

Self-corrections; when a child self-corrects a miscue there is a positive indication of the child's searching and checking procedures. It demonstrates that the child is not satisfied with his/her reading and that the word read aloud is not being confirmed by the cues in the text. Marie Clay (1972) argued that, at least for a time, these miscues are indicative of reading progress. (Later the corrections may occur in the child's head before they are spoken: they therefore become less frequent). Of course, some children may over-correct their reading producing self-corrections for substitutions which produce little or no change in the meaning of the text. Although that does indicate a positive attempt to match reading to text nevertheless the over correction of meaningful miscues may be viewed more negatively as that may not be in the best interests of the reader.

ANALYSING THE MISCUES

We noted above that readers will be making use of the language cue systems as they read. So the *semantic*, or meaning element, of text will be used by readers who will apply their experiences of the world and knowledge about language to aid their reading. The *syntactic*, or sentence construction element will also assist readers. Although readers may not be able to articulate a knowledge of sentence construction, nevertheless their utterances in conversations and discussions will demonstrate the very considerable implicit understanding they have of syntax and which they can apply when reading. There is also the *graphophonic* cue system which readers are able to use when reading. So readers' knowledge of letters (or graphemes) and the associated sounds (or phonemes) support the reading of texts.

At the simplest level of miscue analysis, therefore, we would want to consider each miscue for its syntactic and semantic acceptability and graphophonic appropriateness. For example:

      the   **whistling for**
He saw a boy playing with his dog.

So what can be suggested about each of these miscues? The first miscue, 'the' (a), maintains the syntactic structures and meaning but there is no graphophonic similarity between the text word 'a' and the observed response 'the'. Knowing that the story is about a boy learning to whistle for his dog helps us to understand the next two miscues, 'whistling' (playing) and 'for' (with). Each miscue retains the syntactical structures of the text and maintains the meaning of the story. However there is only partial similarity of a graphophonic nature in the ending of 'whistling' (playing) and none at all in 'for' (with).

If we had wanted to analyse each of those substitutions alongside the reading we could have written it up as:

	syn	sem	g-p
the/a	Y	Y	N
whistling/playing	Y	Y	P
for/with	Y	Y	N

So in response to the questions of syntactic and semantic acceptability and graphophonic appropriateness we have answered Y - Yes, N - No, or P - Partial. Will there be occasions when there is a partial coding for syntactic or semantic acceptability? There will be occasions when we will need to do so. For example;

          Football
He saw a boy playing with his dog.

In that example the reader has maintained sense up to and including the miscue, 'football' (with), but it is not acceptable within the complete sentence. It might therefore be considered as partially acceptable, as would miscues which were acceptable with the last part of the sentence but not the complete sentence.

The analysis of the miscues is therefore based on:

Syntactic acceptability:
Y - miscue syntactically acceptable within complete sentence,
P - miscue acceptable syntactically with first or last part of sentence but not within the complete sentence,
N - miscue is not syntactically acceptable within the sentence.

Semantic acceptability:
Y - miscue semantically acceptable within complete sentence
P - miscue acceptable semantically with first or last part of sentence but not within the complete sentence
N - miscue is not semantically acceptable within the sentence

Graphophonic appropriateness:
Y - high degree of similarity e.g. look/looks, rowing/running
P - some degree of similarity e.g. whistling/playing, hat/horse
N - no degree of similarity e.g. the/a, for/with

It will have become apparent from the short discussion in this section that to consider each miscue on a Yes/No syntactic, semantic, graphophonic basis would be inadequate as it would not account for some of the nuances of difference we have just noted. At the same time it will have become evident that even the Yes/Partial/No analysis will leave some questions unanswered. Clearly there could be a more sophisticated analysis and indeed Kenneth Goodman in one of his earlier procedures scored the graphophonic system on two ten point scales from 0 - 9 (see Appendix D of the Goodman, Watson and Burke, 1987 text). However, for every day use in the classroom that which has been described does appear to be helpful in the majority of situations. After all the teacher is likely to be asking the question "How is this reader getting on with his/her reading? What can I find out about the strategies of the reader?" The teacher may not be aiming to be a researcher; the requirement is for a relatively simple mode of analysis which enables a diagnosis to occur. And, importantly, that analysis provides the basis for the subsequent planning of literacy programmes.

PLANNING LITERACY PROGRAMMES

For the majority of classroom teachers miscue analysis will occur in an informal manner during shared readings. Nevertheless these analyses will help the teacher to assess the strengths and weaknesses of the reader and form the basis for planning future literacy programmes.

In an earlier book (Campbell, 1992) I included a complete transcript of five year old Richard reading to his teacher. A close perusal of that transcript would indicate the full range of miscues that might be produced by a child during a single shared reading. It also suggests the vast amount of information that would be provided by a child who shared a book with a teacher on a regular and frequent basis. The extent of that information can be deduced by considering just the first few lines of the reading by Richard with his teacher:

In the *light* of the moon
the - the
a little egg *lay* on a leaf.
     summers   day
One Sunday morning the warm sun
   out
came up and - pop! - *out* of the egg
a - very Ⓔ
came a tiny and very hungry caterpillar.

looked

He started to look for (some) food.

You will, of course, need to recall that Richard was supported by his teacher during the reading of this story. Indeed the teacher led Richard in the reading of 'light', 'lay' and 'out' with Richard fractionally behind the teacher and echoing the reading of those words. However, in the remainder of the reading it was Richard who was in the lead.

At first sight, and without a knowledge of miscue analysis, one might be inclined to view Richard's reading rather negatively. After all there were seven unexpected responses, and three words where the teacher led the reading, from the text of 41 words. But looked at through the eyes of a miscue analysis the picture becomes more positive:

	syn	sem	g-p
the/a	Y	Y	N
Summer's/Sunday	Y	Y	P
day/morning	Y	Y	N
out/up	Y	Y	P
a very/came	N	N	N
looked/started	P	P	P

In particular the analysis begins to indicate the way in which Richard attempts to maintain the syntax and meaning of the reading. (I recognize that we have only looked at the first six substitutions of Richard's reading, but consider how those miscues, when added to by the rest of this reading and future readings, will enable the teacher to build a comprehensive picture of the child's reading development). Richard appeared to be making less use of the graphophonic cueing system although three of the miscues had some partial similarity between the observed response and the expected response. And later in Richard's reading his miscue of 'pepper' (pears) and his correction to 'pineapples' added some confirmation of a developing attention to the letters and sounds.

The teacher with a day to day knowledge of Richard's miscues and reading development will know far more about his strengths and weaknesses than we can glean from a single miscue analysis. Nevertheless even this limited miscue analysis is suggestive of a five year old who has learnt a great deal about how stories and language work. The teacher will want to build upon those foundations by ensuring that there are opportunities within the print rich classroom for Richard to hear stories read aloud, to engage in frequent shared readings, to have opportunities for silent reading and to be given the opportunity to write every day for real purposes. These literacy activities would be enhanced by home-school links which encourage a shared involvement in Richard's reading development. More specifically the teacher might decide to place greater emphasis upon the use of nursery rhymes in the classroom in order to encourage phonemic awareness. ("Please teach children nursery rhymes, and the phonology will come, noticed with fun." Meek, 1990. p. 151). The teacher will want to check upon the child's invented spellings in his writing, and future miscues during oral reading, in order to determine that there is a growth in the understanding and use of the graphophonic cueing system while maintaining an emphasis upon meaning.

Miscue analysis can be used by teachers in their day to day interactions with children during literacy activities. But the object of miscue analysis is not just for teachers to become skilled in the technique but to allow them to assess and evaluate the childrens' development. That evaluation gives a basis for a consideration of the range of literacy activities that are provided in the classroom. Miscue analysis leads to evaluation and planning. It can also lead to a more considered response, by the teacher, to the miscues that are produced during a shared reading.

RESPONDING TO MISCUES

One of the regular and frequent teaching activities of the primary school classroom is shared reading, or hearing children read. The teacher, the child and the book are, of course, central to the interaction. During these interactions the teacher will hope to serve a number of purposes. In particular, the teacher will wish to develop or maintain an interest in books and establish an enjoyable read for the child. For some children the teacher might provide a model of the reading before the child attempts to read with the teacher in support. But what would be the nature of that support?

As a support and guide for the child the teacher would work to a number of principles. First, the teacher would want to encourage the child as an active and constructive learner. That means that the teacher would want to remain in the background as much as possible. Therefore, when the child miscues the teacher would wait to give time for the child to think about the miscue, the text and the reading. Second, when the teacher gives support it would be in a format that provides minimal disruption to the child away from the text. An objective will be to maintain a focus upon the book. Third, the teacher will wish to place the emphasis upon a meaningful reading. Therefore the nature of the miscue will in part determine the kind of support that the teacher gives. (In part, because the teacher's knowledge of the child, the text and the miscue will be considered before the teacher responds).

Because the teacher will wish to encourage the notion of reading as being concerned with meaning, when the child produces a meaningful miscue (with syntactic and semantic appropriateness) the teacher may decide not to respond at all. However, if the miscue distorts the syntax/semantics then the teacher may provide some support. That support might be simply to restart the sentence for the child and to read up to the miscue, an approach we might refer to as word cueing. This strategy is offered with a rising intonation which brings the child back into the reading. On those occasions where the miscue is of the first word in the sentence then the teacher is unable to use a word-cueing strategy and I have noted that many teachers use a soft non-punitive negative feedback, i.e. they say 'no', but gently. Of course, at times in order to get the reader back on track, especially where the miscue is not meaningful, the teacher might simply provide the word. However, although this creates very little disruption to the reading it does not keep the child actively involved with the text. The teacher will wish, therefore, to use this strategy sparingly.

On a few occasions the teacher may decide to follow the child's use of the graphophonic cueing system to confirm, for instance, the use of the first letter(s) in a miscue: a phonic analysis strategy. Of course, by concentrating upon the letters in a word the child's attention is taken away momentarily from the whole text. This strategy will also be used sparingly because it disrupts the flow of reading. (The analysis of Richard's reading in Campbell (1992) includes a more complete debate of the teacher's response to miscues).

Of course, there is always a danger in suggesting particular strategies to be used by the teacher in response to miscues. This lies in the simple and almost mechanistic use of the strategies. The strategies, and more especially the principles, may act as a useful guide for the teacher. However, what teachers must do is to use these in relation to the context and children with whom they are working and then base their support upon professional judgements.

RETELLING

Although I have concentrated upon the miscues made during an oral reading a formal miscue analysis (or a shared reading) might also include a retelling of the story by the child. That retelling would have been signalled by the teacher, at the beginning of the session, by indicating to the reader that after the reading they would be asked to tell everything that could be remembered of the story. Furthermore in a formal miscue analysis the story retelling can be scored: either for attention to characters and events, using a 0-100 point scale (Goodman, Watson and Burke, 1987) or for straight recall, overall structure and appreciation using a 1-3 point scale linked to levels of understanding (Arnold,1984).

In the context of everyday classroom activities the teacher might be more inclined to use a retelling during shared readings, but not on each occasion and not scored in a detailed manner. But retellings can be useful to the teacher because they provide additional information about the child's understanding of and involvement with the text. During retellings the teacher would expect the child to tell about the characters, setting and plot, within a beginning, middle and end. Therefore the child would be demonstrating some understanding of story grammar. The child might also express some feelings toward the story, and this would be encouraged by the teacher because it would indicate that a reflective reading had occurred.

Much of the retelling would be produced by the child unaided. But the teacher might need to encourage the reader to make text-to-life connections, to comment upon the illustrations and the author and perhaps to discuss future book selections. Of course in an aided retelling the teacher will need to avoid turning the event into a quiz. Not all of the child's knowledge about a book might be revealed during a single retelling. But these retellings will provide further information for the teacher about the child's development as a reader.

As a child develops towards independence as a reader it might be that the classroom shared readings become almost solely concerned with retelling. Oral reading becomes less productive for the child and less informative for the teacher. So retellings can be used firstly to supplement the miscue information acquired during an oral reading and secondly, as a major source of information about more independent readers.

CRITICISMS OF MISCUE ANALYSIS

Teachers find that once they have been introduced to and absorbed some of the principles and details of miscue analysis then their listening to a child read is changed. It is changed to a more analytic mode which asks: Why did the reader produce that miscue? What does that tell me about this child as a reader? (The teacher has developed what Yetta Goodman (Goodman & Goodman 1991) refers to as a "miscue head" namely a scheme of miscue analysis in the head). These changes are constructive because the teacher now can gain additional information about the child as a developing reader.

However, despite these constructive and professional changes, the teacher will be aware on occasions of difficulties. These difficulties have been articulated in a number of critical comments by researchers. Hood (1978), for instance, doubted the value of miscue analysis for classroom teachers as it is very time consuming when used in a formal manner. Leu (1981) was concerned in particular about the source of multiple source miscues. (Think again about Richard's 'Summer's' (Sunday) miscue, our assessment of that miscue suggested the use of syntactic, semantic and graphophonic cueing systems but we do not know for sure - Richard may have used just one or a combination of cues). It was a somewhat similar area that concerned Potter (1980) who suggested, from a study of children reading words in and out of context, that a child might use the graphophonic word ending cue to read a single, out of context, word and produce a response which would appear to give that word syntactic acceptability. Leu noted also the influence of text difficulty on the miscues produced and we will return to that issue in the next section.

Interestingly although critiques have been made of miscue analysis each author appeared to want to add a positive foot note such as not wishing to question the usefulness of miscue analysis. So where does that leave the classroom teacher? Firstly, the Hood critique regarding time will be of least concern, because what this text has been arguing is the need for the teacher to know about miscue analysis so that it becomes part of them (the miscue head). Therefore, each shared reading during normal classroom activities becomes a more analytic activity. Secondly, the other concerns would be of more importance if the teacher was evaluating on the basis of a single miscue analysis. However, as the teacher will be analysing several readings, whether formally or by just noting important features in the mind, the amount of data collected will give confidence to the analysis that is made.

TEXT AND TEACHER INFLUENCES ON CHILDREN'S MISCUES

When a teacher is sharing a book with a young reader the miscues produced by that reader will give information about the child's strengths and strategies as a reader. However, in part, those miscues that are produced might also be giving some information about the text being read and/or the teaching strategies that are adopted by the teacher (or that have been adopted by other teachers/significant adults in recent literacy activities). So how will the text and the teacher influence the miscues that are produced?

Where the text is very difficult for the reader or where the text lacks predictability the reader will find it problematic to use the contextual cues of syntax and semantics. The miscues that are produced might then suggest a considerable use of the graphophonic cue system. And in those circumstances a young reader might produce a large number of nonwords.

Where the books being read by the young reader are drawn from a reading scheme many of the substitutions might be constrained by an additional feature. The substitutions, while being linked to syntactic, semantic and graphophonic cues, will often be words which have been previously read. In other words the child will have recognized the use of repetition in reading schemes. Therefore while using the language cues the child will also be trying to recall a word that has previously occurred in the scheme.

The teacher needs to be aware of the influence of the text upon the miscues produced. Occasionally there will be a need for the teacher to encourage the reader towards a more predictable book, where the context cues will be more readily accessible.

During a formal miscue analysis the influence of the teacher might be less obvious. However even there it might still be noted. If the teacher or other adults had encouraged the child to think about letters and sounds it should not surprise us if miscues of sounding-out and/or nonwords figured prominently in the observed responses.

During shared readings the teacher will, of course, be supporting the reader. However, that support will occasionally be reflected in the miscues produced by the reader. For instance in an earlier text (Campbell,1988) I reported where a child, Jason, had apparently opted out of the reading because he knew that his hesitations would be followed almost immediately by the teacher giving the word. So Jason adopted the role of hesitator and encouraged his teacher to become the reader!

Earlier in this booklet, we considered a short part of Richard's reading. You will recall that that reading was produced during a shared reading with a teacher. The last line that I presented included a 'looked' (started) substitution miscue in the sentence 'He started to look for some food'. However, if we consider that miscue in the context of the interaction a different perspective emerges:

Teacher: What did he start to do?
Richard: He looked (started)

Was the miscue, 'looked', a substitution for the text word 'started'? Or, had Richard used the teacher's introduction to the new page, and used the question including the word 'start' to by-pass the word 'started'? I cannot give an answer to the question, but I do recognize that during shared reading interactions some of the miscues that are produced are influenced by the teacher's contribution to the interaction.

None of the above invalidates the use of miscue analysis to gain an insight into a child's reading. However, it does emphasise the attention and skill with which a teacher should handle a shared reading interaction. It also indicates the need to evaluate a miscue analysis with great care especially when that analysis has been carried out informally as part of a classroom literacy activity and where that analysis is being used by the teacher to develop an assessment of the child as a reader.

RUNNING RECORDS

Not only will teachers be carrying out informal miscue analyses during shared readings, but they will also be involved with a variant of that procedure, namely running records, at other times. The impetus for working with running records comes from two sources. First, the work of Marie Clay (1985) in developing and popularising the Reading Recovery programme has encouraged teachers to consider the use of running records which forms part of the diagnostic element of that programme. Second, those teachers who are responsible for Year 2 classes in England and Wales will have been required to use running records as part of the assessment process at Key Stage 1 of the National Curriculum (SEAC, 1992). (And those Key Stage 1 teachers would be able to do so more effectively if they had a knowledge not just of running records but also of miscue analysis. Because in the assessment the teacher is instructed to tell a word where *meaning* is being lost and words told are instrumental in the scoring).

A running record, if applied to the first few lines of Richard's reading, would be presented as:

In the light of the moon	T / T / / /
a little egg lay on a leaf	the-the T / / / / /
One Sunday morning the warm	/ Summer's day / /
sun came up and pop out of the egg	/ / out / / T / / /
came a tiny and very hungry caterpillar.	a very(T) / / / / / /
He started to look for some food.	/looked-starts/ / /O /

(*Conventions*

/	word read correctly
T	word told by the teacher
the	substituted word
looked-starts	substitution sequence
O	omission of word
SC	would be used to indicate a self-correction.)

In many senses the running record represents another way of coding a miscue analysis, although it is argued that an advantage of a running record is that it can be completed at any time on a plain sheet of paper, i.e. it does not require a duplicated sheet of the text or a tape recording of the reading. However, the important issue is not that the teacher becomes a skilled coder but that the information that is made available from that coding can be used to diagnose a child's strengths and weaknesses. And that implies an awareness and knowledge of the language cue systems that the child is using in his/her reading.

Marie Clay (1985) suggests that once the teacher is able take running records then the miscues can be considered for the cues used by the child: S for structure, M for meaning and V for visual. However that analysis can be seen to link very directly to the syntactic, semantic and graphophonic analysis system that we have debated earlier. Nevertheless, whichever system is used, the important feature is that we are learning more about the child as a reader.

For instance, using the limited information from the first six lines of Richard's reading the teacher would have been able to have recorded, as many teachers do, in a simple but helpful format:

Richard	S	M	V
Very Hungry Caterpillar	Good use	Maintained meaning	Evidence of /S-/ /-ed/

Therefore Richard's good use of structure and meaning and his limited use of visual cues can be noted. More specifically the teacher would have been able to have noted, as part of the assessment, Richard's apparent use of the first letter s- and the word ending -ed even within this short reading.

RETROSPECTIVE MISCUE ANALYSIS

From all that has been argued in this text it will be apparent that young readers bring to the task of reading an implicit knowledge and understanding of the language cue systems. Nevertheless, for whatever reasons, a number of children may not develop adequately as readers. In some circumstances it might be beneficial if such readers could be made more aware, and explicitly so, of their reading strategies. Retrospective miscue analysis (RMA) is a procedure which enables that to happen.

Ann Marek (1989, 1991), working with Kenneth and Yetta Goodman, has developed that procedure while working with adults who were unable to read the materials that they wished, or needed, to read. It might also be suitable for work with adolescents struggling with their reading. The starting point for using RMA has to be a teacher who is confident in the use of miscue analysis and therefore able to encourage a reader to reflect upon and self-evaluate their own reading.

RMA starts with the collection of an oral reading miscue analysis in a normal fashion. The teacher then analyses the reader's miscues and selects a small number of miscues for discussion at a later time (5 miscues could take as long as twenty minutes to discuss). Because these readers will often perceive their reading to be ineffective it may be important to select miscues, especially initially, which demonstrate effective reading strategies. Therefore miscues which were syntactically and semantically acceptable and were uncorrected or those which were unacceptable and were corrected can provide a good starting point.

Among the suggestions of questions for the teacher to ask the reader, Marek in both her articles, lists the following:
1) Does the miscue make sense?
2) Was the miscue corrected? Should it have been?
3) Does the miscue look like what was on the page?
4) Does the miscue sound like what was on the page?
5) Why do you think you made the miscue?
6) Did the miscue affect your understanding of the text?

Of course, questions 3 and 4 may encourage the use of the graphophonic cues rather than emphasising meaning. Therefore it will be the teacher's knowledge of the reader and the strategies used by that reader which will guide the teacher in the selection of the miscues for discussion and which of the questions to be used during that discussion.

So what are the benefits of RMA? In particular the self-reflection and self-evaluation which is encouraged by retrospective miscue analysis can be instrumental in increasing the self-confidence of the reader. But initial research in this area suggests that it might do more than that, because it also helps the reader to understand more fully how to tackle new reading material and which strategies to adopt when confronted by difficulties. Such outcomes would suggest a place for RMA with older readers.

MISCUE ANALYSIS IN MORE DETAIL

The more frequently a teacher uses miscue analysis, or asks 'Why did the reader produce that miscue?' during a shared reading, the more knowledgeable is that teacher likely to become about miscue analysis. And that knowledge will raise questions about the nature of miscue analysis and certainly about the simple, albeit useful, mode of analysing miscues in the classroom which was suggested earlier.

In the earlier section we coded for graphophonic appropriateness using the categories of high, some and no degree of similarity. That simple coding might be questioned. For instance the examples I gave for some degree of similarity were whistling/playing and hat/horse. In the first the similarity is in the word ending and in the second in the word beginning. Should they be regarded as equal? And should we be considering the words graphophonically rather than first for graphic similarity and second for phonemic similarity? As I indicated earlier, Kenneth Goodman (Appendix D, Goodman, Watson and Burke, 1987) had a procedure for considering graphic proximity and phonemic proximity both on a ten point scale from 0 - 9. On those scales the beginning of words is scored more highly than word endings so our two examples would be scored 3 and 4 respectively. Of course, it is not the actual score that is important so much as being aware of the levels of discrimination being demonstrated by the child.

There are other areas which will be noted as the teacher becomes more familiar with miscue analysis. For instance although semantic acceptability will indicate the extent to which the miscue has maintained meaning within the sentence there will be occasions when, although the miscue is acceptable semantically, there is a meaning change from the author's apparent intention. There will also be readings when dialect will play a major part in the miscues that are produced and teachers will have to be sensitive to those miscues, especially if they are responding to them during a shared reading. And self-corrections is an area which provides important insights into the child's confirming strategies and might therefore be an area for separate detailed consideration by the teacher.

Whether the questions raised in this section are of importance to the classroom teacher I leave to each reader of this book to answer. But an initial knowledge of miscue analysis appears to lead to further questions about the nuances of the analysis. Nevertheless what many teachers with whom I have worked have suggested is that miscue analysis, in whatever form, has a profound influence upon their teaching. It does so because it seems to allow for a more insightful and analytic assessment of the child's development as a reader.

REFERENCES

Arnold, H. (1982) *Listening to Children Reading*. London: Hodder and Stoughton.

Arnold, H. (1984) *Making Sense of It*. London: Hodder and Stoughton.

Campbell, R. (1988) *Hearing Children Read*. London: Routledge.

Campbell, R. (1992) *Reading Real Books*. Buckingham: Open University Press.

Clay, M.M. (1972) *Reading: The Patterning of Complex Behaviour*. London: Heinemann.

Clay, M. M. (1985) *The Early Detection of Reading Difficulties*. Auckland: Heinemann Educational.

Goodman, K. (1973) 'Miscues: Windows on the Reading Process'. In Gollasch, F. V. (1982) *Language and Literacy: The Selected Writings of Kenneth S. Goodman*. London: Routledge.

Goodman, K. & Goodman, Y. (1991) 'Knowing students as readers: Miscue Analysis'. In Goodman, K., Bird, L. & Goodman, Y. (1991) *The Whole Language Catalog*. Santa Rosa, Calif: American School Publishers.

Goodman, Y., Watson, D. & Burke, C. (1987) *Reading Miscue Inventory: Alternative Procedures*. New York: Richard C. Owen Publishers Inc.

Hood, J. (1978) 'Is miscue analysis practical for teachers?' *The Reading Teacher*. 32(3) pp. 260-266.

Leu, J. (1982) 'Oral reading error analysis: A critical review of research and application'. *Reading Research Quarterly*. 17(3) pp. 420-437.

Marek, A. (1989) 'Using evaluation as an instructional strategy for adult readers'. In Goodman, K., Goodman, Y. and Hood, W. (1989) *The Whole Language Evaluation Book*. Portsmouth, New Hampshire: Heinemann.

Marek, A. (1991) 'Retrospective Miscue Analysis: An instructional strategy for revaluing the reading process'. In Goodman, K., Bird, L. and Goodman, Y. (1991) *The Whole Language Catalog*. Santa Rosa, Calif: American School Publishers.

Meek, M. (1990) 'What do we know about reading that helps us teach?' In Carter, R. (1990) *Knowledge about Language and the Curriculum: The LINC Reader*. London: Hodder & Stoughton.

Potter, F. (1980) 'Miscue analysis: a cautionary note'. *Journal of Research in Reading*. 3(2) pp. 116-128.

SEAC (1992) *Standard Assessment Task: Teacher's Handbook. Key Stage 1*. London: HMSO.

ABOUT THE AUTHOR

Robin Campbell studied for his Teaching Certificate at Borough Road College, Middlesex and then taught in primary, mainly, and secondary schools for fifteen years. He was headteacher of a primary school directly before moving into teacher education.

As a primary school teacher he had shared books with many children on an individual basis, and after gaining degrees with the Open University, 'Hearing children read' became the focus for his PhD thesis at London University. Subsequently he has had books published on 'Hearing Children Read' (1988) Routledge, 'Reading Together' (1990) Open University Press, and 'Reading Real Books' (1992) Open University Press. His book 'Reading Together' received the 1991 Donald Moyle UKRA award. In each of those books miscue analysis informed part of the writing.

Currently Robin Campbell is Professor of Primary Education at the University of Hertfordshire. He is also the review editor for the UKRA journal 'Reading'.